Discover Jesus

Investigating Christian Belief

By Mike Treneer

First paperback edition printed 2018 in the United Kingdom

A catalogue record for this book is available from the British Library

ISBN 978-1-900964-31-9

Published by Navigators UK (www.navigators.co.uk)

"To advance the gospel of Jesus and his kingdom into the nations through spiritual generations of labourers living and discipling among the lost."

What we share are not merely words, but words that have transformed us, and can transform those we walk with. We share life to life, engaging with Jesus through his Word and prayer. Our aim is not mere knowledge or spirituality, but his transformation by his Spirit. It does not end with us, but goes on to the next spiritual generation, and on to succeeding generations.

Organisationally the Navigators is a worldwide mission partnership existing in over a hundred countries. Navigators UK is a registered charity and is a member of both the Evangelical Alliance and Global Connections. Navigators UK has been serving in the UK for 60 years.

Contents

Introduction

What's this book about?

This book contains a series of five Bible studies designed to help people look for themselves at the basics of the Christian faith using the original source material, the Bible.

We are inviting you to study the Bible because of its claim to be the definitive record of God making himself known to people, and also because we ourselves, along with many others, have come face to face with the living God in its pages.

Why bother?

"A close study of the remarkable collection of books which are known as the New Testament can, and constantly does, challenge, provoke and appeal at a deeper level and with more profound authority than any other human writing. Human beings can easily insulate themselves from any shock or disturbance of this kind by simply not reading it… It means that the most important event in history is politely and quietly bypassed. For it is not as though the evidence has been examined and found unconvincing; it had simply never been examined." [1]

Hopefully these studies will give people an opportunity to remedy this situation, to consider the evidence of the New Testament for themselves and to come to a considered conclusion about its message.

The five studies in this series explore what the Bible says about Truth, God, Us, Christ and Trust.

Why this type of approach?

Our aim is to encourage you not only to look into the Bible but also to think about what it says. Please do not feel limited by the references given and the questions covered. Obviously it will help you most to read as much of the New Testament as possible, but we have assumed you are limited for time and have therefore tried to suggest the most relevant passages.

The Bible references are given in the form 'John 3:16', which is the book of John, chapter 3, verse 16.

[1] J.B. Phillips, *Ring of Truth: A Translator's Testimony* (Hodder and Stoughton, 1978)

Truth

"'What is faith?' asked the teacher. A young boy answered in a flash: 'Believing something you know isn't true.'" ²

Is faith a leap in the dark? Does it involve some form of intellectual suicide? Or is faith being convinced beyond reasonable doubt by facts?

The facts of the matter

Christian belief is based on the historical events surrounding the life of Jesus Christ, events that are both startling and unique. The claim is made, both by the nature of these events and by the people who witnessed them, that God himself has stepped into human history. Clearly much is at stake and an honest and unbiased look at the facts must be the launching point for an investigation of Christian belief.

At no point are the facts harder to accept, or of more consequence, than when it comes to the resurrection of Jesus.

> "[Jesus Christ] was appointed the Son of God in power by his resurrection from the dead" (Romans 1:4)

The testimony of John the Apostle

Read John 19:31 – 20:31.

The testimony of Luke

Luke, who was a doctor, was the writer of Luke's Gospel and Acts. In Luke 24 and the early chapters of Acts, Luke records several further details about the resurrection.

Q1   (a)   What was the disciples' initial reaction? Luke 24:10-11

(b)   What caused them to think again? Luke 24:36-43

(c)   How did they become convinced? Acts 1:3

(d)   What was the result? Acts 4:18-20, Acts 5:40-42

(e)   How many people were convinced about the resurrection within the first few weeks? Acts 2:41, Acts 4:4

The testimony of Paul

Paul was formerly a bitter enemy of the early Christians. His autobiography can be found in Acts 26:9-18.

Read 1 Corinthians 15:3-9.

Q2   How could Paul's statements have been checked?

Responses to the resurrection

Q3   (a)   What was the official Jewish explanation? Matthew 28:11-15

        (b)   What was the reaction of the Greeks? Acts 17:18-21, 32

(c)   What was the eyewitness explanation? Acts 5:27-32

(d)   What possible explanations can you think of for the empty tomb?

Q4   (a)   Why do you think the resurrection is important to the Christian faith?

(b)   What follows from believing that Jesus Christ rose from the dead?

(c)   What is your personal response to the resurrection, and why?

"As a lawyer I have made a prolonged study of the evidences for [the resurrection of Jesus Christ]. To me the evidence is conclusive, and over and over again in the High Court I have secured a verdict on evidence not nearly so compelling... The Gospel evidence for the resurrection ... I accept unreservedly as the testimony of truthful men to facts they were able to substantiate." [3]

But are these 'facts' that the Bible presents reliable?

For after all, "The heart cannot delight in what the mind rejects as false." [4]

There are two important questions we must answer:

- How reliable is the Bible? Is what we read in our Bibles the same as the apostles originally wrote, or has it been embellished and exaggerated over the years?
- If this is what the apostles wrote, were they deliberately lying, or deceived by someone else's lies? Or was this a story they never intended to be taken literally?

How reliable is the Bible?

F.F. Bruce, formerly Rylands Professor of Biblical Criticism and Exegesis at Manchester University, says:

> "There is no body of ancient literature in the world which enjoys such a wealth of textual attestation as the New Testament." [5]

For example, Caesar's Gallic Wars, written in 58-50 BC, exists in ten manuscripts, the oldest of which dates from AD 900. And yet no serious scholar doubts that they are genuine. In contrast, the New Testament, which was written in AD 48-100, exists in about 5000 Greek manuscripts and thousands more in Latin, Syriac and other languages. The best and most important date from about AD 350, but other fragments date from as early as AD 120. It is not surprising then that Sir Frederick Kenyon, who was director and principal librarian of the British Museum, says:

> "The interval then between the date of original composition and the earliest extant evidence becomes so small as to be in fact negligible, and the last foundation for any doubt that the Scriptures have come down to us substantially as they were written has now been removed. Both the authenticity and the general integrity of the books of the New Testament may be regarded as finally established." [6]

What was the intention of the Bible writers?

Q5 According to the following passages, what was the intention of the writers?

Luke 1:1-4

1 John 1:1-4

Q6 What did they claim about their message?

John 19:35, 21:24

Acts 26:24-26

2 Peter 1:16

Q7   What standard of integrity did they uphold?

Colossians 3:9

Pliny the Younger, Governor of Bithynia, wrote to the Emperor Trajan in AD 112 seeking advice on how to treat Christians. He explained that he had been killing them as a matter of course, but was not sure what they were guilty of. He told how they regularly…

> "…bound themselves to a solemn oath, not to any wicked deeds, but never to commit any fraud, theft, adultery, never to falsify their word, not to deny a trust when they should be called upon to deliver it up." [7]

Over fifty times in the New Testament the writers describe their message as 'the truth'. The events they wrote about were by their very nature out of the ordinary. The writers themselves were clearly aware that they were recording events that were both unique and tremendously important.

Q8   Ask yourself: Were the New Testament writers lying? Were they deceived? Or were they telling the truth?

Further reading

If you are interested in finding out more about the historical reliability of the New Testament and the evidence for the resurrection of Jesus, we recommend the following books:

- Amy Orr-Ewing, *Why Trust the Bible? Answers to 10 Tough Questions* (IVP, 2008)
- F.F. Bruce, *The New Testament Documents: Are They Reliable?* (IVP, 2000)
- Val Grieve, *Your Verdict on the Empty Tomb* (Evangelical Press, 2017)
- Frank Morison, *Who Moved the Stone?* (Authentic Media, 2006)
- Tim Keller, *The Reason for God: Belief in an Age of Scepticism* (Hodder & Stoughton, 2009)

[2] Paul E. Little, *Know Why You Believe* (IVP, 2008)

[3] Edward Clarke, quoted in John Stott, *Basic Christianity* (IVP, 2013)

[4] Clark Pinnock, *Set Forth Your Case: An Examination of Christianity* (Moody Publishers, 2000)

[5] F.F. Bruce, *The Books and the Parchments* (Zondervan, 1991)

[6] Frederic Kenyon, *The Bible and Archaeology* (George G. Harrap, 1949)

[7] Pliny the Younger, Epistles X:96

Tim's Story

When I turned up to university, I had no idea how to connect the life I was living Monday to Saturday with what I said I believed on a Sunday morning. No wonder I was making poor decisions with my time, money, friendships and university experience. But all that began to change when an older guy started meeting with me, and helping me learn how to read the Bible in a way that was startlingly relevant. I began to see that my life was being changed by the stories, by the truths, and by the God that I came to know through its pages. Reading the Bible like this was an invitation to build my life on something. It was an invitation to live my life for something. It was an invitation to live life the way it was meant to be lived. And one of the most animating questions for my life now is, "How can I experience this life more fully, and help others do the same?"

God

"In the beginning God..." (Genesis 1:1)

Some people claim that there is no God. Some say there might be, but we can never know. Some cannot bear even to think about it. Others claim that there is a God and that he can be known, loved, trusted and worshipped.

Is there a God?

No question carries more consequences for our lives than this.

How could we know?

Some people claim that even if God exists, we finite beings cannot discover or understand the infinite. But Christians believe that God has taken the initiative.

Q1 How does the Bible describe the way God made himself known? Hebrews 1:1-2

"No one has ever seen God, but the one and only Son, who is himself God and is in closest relationship with the Father, has made him known." (John 1:18)

Q2 According to the Bible, why has God revealed himself in this way? John 3:16

Christians believe that God has revealed himself, so they primarily point to God's self-revelation as evidence for his existence and character.

Weighing the evidence

Q3 (a) What positive reasons do you think an atheist might give for believing in the non-existence of God?

(b) What reasons could a Christian give for believing in God?

You may like to look at Hebrews 1:1-2, Romans 1:20, John 14:8-11, Acts 17:31 and Romans 2:13-14.

You could also consider the wonder of creation:

> "My religion consists of a humble admiration of the illimitable superior spirit who reveals himself in the slight details we are able to perceive with our frail and feeble minds. That deeply emotional conviction of the presence of a superior reasoning power which is revealed in the incomprehensible Universe forms my idea of God." (Albert Einstein) [8]

And the test of experience:

> "For I cried to him and he answered me! He freed me from all my fears. Others too were radiant at what he did for them... This poor man cried to the Lord – and the Lord heard him and saved him out of his troubles… Oh, put God to the test and see how kind he is! See for yourself the way his mercies shower down on all who trust in him." (written by David, King of Israel, circa 1000 BC; Psalm 34:4-8 TLB)

 What do you consider to be the most compelling evidence for the existence or the non-existence of God, and why?

What is he like?

The living God

> "God is a spirit, infinite, eternal and unchangeable in his being, wisdom, power, holiness, justice, goodness and truth." [9]

 Read Acts 17:22-31 and see how the Apostle Paul describes God to a pagan audience. Note one thing about God from each verse.

v 24   v 28

v 25   v 29

v 26   v 30

v 27   v 31

"[People] are reluctant to pass over from the notion of an abstract and negative deity to the living God. I do not wonder. The Pantheist's God does nothing, demands nothing. He is there if you wish for Him, like a book on the shelf, He will not pursue you... But God Himself, alive... There comes a moment when people who have been dabbling in religion ('man's search for God'!) suddenly draw back. Supposing we really found Him? We never meant it to come to that! Worse still suppose He had found us." [10]

The loving God

"Whoever does not love does not know God, because God is love." (1 John 4:8)

"Sentimental ideas of His love as an indulgent, benevolent softness, divorced from moral standards and concerns must be ruled out... God's love is holy love... It expresses holiness in the lover and seeks holiness in the beloved." [11]

Q6 How does Jesus Christ describe God in the following verses?

Luke 6:35-36

Matthew 7:11

Matthew 5:48

Q7 Consider the following Old Testament passages. What word would you use to summarise the aspect of God's character displayed in each passage?

(a) "The Lord is gracious and compassionate, slow to anger and rich in love. The Lord is good to all; he has compassion on all he has made." (Psalm 145:8-9)

(b) "For you are not a God who is pleased with wickedness; with you, evil people are not welcome. The arrogant cannot stand in your presence. You hate all who do wrong; you destroy those who tell lies. The bloodthirsty and deceitful you, Lord, detest." (Psalm 5:4-6)

Q8   How does God display his love?

Acts 17:25

Romans 5:8

2 Peter 3:7-9 (especially v 9)

"You must try to appreciate both the kindness and strict justice of God."
(Romans 11:22 J.B. Phillips)

The holy God

"Be holy because I, the Lord your God, am holy." (Leviticus 19:2)

The word 'holy' means 'set apart'. It stresses the purity of God. He is completely and utterly good; his record and conscience are spotless. It would be impossible for him to ever associate himself with something that goes against his perfect standards.

Q9   How do Jesus' statements in Matthew 7:21-23 demonstrate God's holiness?

Q10   How would you express what Revelation 15:3-4 teaches us about God?

Some people are confused by an apparently different God in the Old and New Testaments. The Old Testament, presenting God's law, stresses his holiness, while the New Testament, presenting God's Son, stresses his love. But throughout the Bible, whichever aspect of God's character is being stressed, both his great love and his great holiness are on display.

"Righteousness and justice are the foundation of your throne; love and faithfulness go before you." (Psalm 89:14)

Q11 What are the consequences for us of God's holiness?

Romans 1:18

Romans 14:10-12

So what?

Q12 What must we be careful to avoid? Romans 2:4-5

Q13 What response does God look for in us?

Acts 17:27

Acts 17:30

Hebrews 11:6

Mark 12:30

Q14 How can we know him? John 14:6-7

"Now this is eternal life: that they know you, the only true God, and Jesus Christ, whom you have sent." (John 17:3)

Further reading

- Michael Ots, *What Kind of God?* (IVP, 2016)
- Jen Wilkin, *None Like Him: 10 Ways God is Different from Us (and Why That's a Good Thing)* (Crossway Books, 2016)
- C.S. Lewis, *Mere Christianity* (William Collins, 2016)

Although in this section we haven't tackled the questions raised by human suffering and the existence of evil, this does not mean the Bible has nothing to say on these issues. If you'd like to explore these topics, we suggest the following books:

- C.S. Lewis, *The Problem of Pain* (William Collins, 2015)
- J.W. Wenham, *The Goodness of God* (IVP, 1974)

[8] 'The Universe and Dr Einstein', p. 85, William Sloane Associates, quoted in Paul E. Little, *Know Why You Believe* (IVP, 2008)

[9] *Westminster Shorter Catechism* (see John 4:24, Job 11:7-9, Psalm 90:2, James 1:17, Psalm 147:5, Revelation 4:8 and 15:4, Exodus 34:6-7)

[10] C.S. Lewis, *Miracles* (William Collins, 2016)

[11] J.I. Packer, *Knowing God* (Hodder and Stoughton, 2005)

Eva's Story

When I was 17 I overheard someone speaking to a man about Jesus. The man shook his head and said, "If you are going to tell me about God, let me ask you a question. Have you ever read the Bible from cover to cover? If not, don't preach to me. How can Christians say they know God, when they don't even know what the Bible says about God?"

That got my attention and I began to read my Bible from the beginning to the end. By the time I was 23 I had read it five times. But reading the Bible did much more for me than becoming a tool for telling others about God, it became God's personal letter to me.

I read the Bible to meet with my Father, to learn from Jesus, and to be comforted by the Spirit. I meditate on the Bible to go deep into God. Through it I have learned how wonderful he is, how far above my comprehension he is. The Bible is the guide of my life, living words that come from our living God.

Us

"Then God said, 'Let us make mankind in our image...'" (Genesis 1:26)

"For man is not just a chance configuration of atoms in the slipstream of meaningless chance history. No. Man made in the image of God has a purpose - to be in relationship to the God who is there." [12]

Who am I? Where am I going? Is there a purpose and meaning for my life? And if there is a God of love, why do I not experience him and see his love more clearly in the world?

A real purpose for life

"So God created mankind in his own image, in the image of God he created them; male and female he created them. God blessed them and said to them, 'Be fruitful and increase in number; fill the earth and subdue it. Rule over the fish in the sea and the birds in the sky and over every living creature that moves on the ground.' ... And it was so. God saw all that he had made, and it was very good. And there was evening, and there was morning – the sixth day." (Genesis 1:27-31)

Q1 According to Acts 17:26-27, why did God make human beings?

This truth is expressed in the short but profound statement of the *Westminster Shorter Catechism*:

"[Humanity's] chief end is to glorify God, and to enjoy him forever." [13]

Q2 What is God's ultimate purpose for people? Revelation 21:3-4

"I have come that they may have life, and have it to the full." (John 10:10)

Q3 What does Jesus say are God's two greatest purposes for men and women? Matthew 22:35-40

Q4 How do the above statements from the Bible compare with what you consider to be your purpose for life?

The first purpose rejected: we don't love God

> "Whatever else is or is not true, this one thing is certain – man is not what he was meant to be." [14]

Genesis 3:1-13 tells of the initial disobedience and rejection of God's purposes by men and women, which has continued throughout human history. The result for all of us is that we do not think straight about God, we do not by nature love God and we do not choose God's way above all else.

 Q5 The following Bible passage describes a typical human response to God:

> "I gave them this command: Obey me, and I will be your God and you will be my people. Walk in obedience to all I command you, that it may go well with you. But they did not listen or pay attention; instead, they followed the stubborn inclinations of their evil hearts. They went backward and not forward… Again and again I sent you my servants the prophets. But they did not listen to me or pay attention. They were stiff-necked…" (Jeremiah 7:23-26)

(a) According to this passage, what was God's intention for people?

(b) What was their response?

(c) How did God respond when they would not listen?

(d) What was the result?

 Q6 "Then the man and his wife heard the sound of the Lord God as he was walking in the garden in the cool of the day, and they hid from the Lord God among the trees of the garden. But the Lord God called to the man, 'Where are you?'" (Genesis 3:8-9)

In what ways do people hide from God today?

Q7 Read Romans 1:18-32.

    (a)   How does Paul describe people's behaviour toward God?
                (see especially verses 21, 25 and 28)

    (b)   What is the result?

The Bible clearly states that people's rejection of God is motivated by moral rather than philosophical or scientific issues. This is illustrated by the following statement of Aldous Huxley:

> "I had motives for not wanting the world to have a meaning; consequently assumed that it had none, and was able without any difficulty to find satisfying reasons for this assumption. The philosopher who finds no meaning in the world is not concerned exclusively with a problem in pure metaphysics; he is also concerned to prove that there is no valid reason why he personally should not do as he wants to do, or why his friends should not seize political power and govern in the way that they find most advantageous to themselves… For myself, the philosophy of meaninglessness was essentially an instrument of liberation, sexual and political." [15]

The second purpose rejected: we don't love one another

Q8 How does God tell us to behave toward one another? Colossians 3:12-14
(Try to express the thoughts in your own words; this will help you to think about what is meant.)

Q9   (a)   In contrast to this, how do people tend to behave toward one another in practice? Romans 1:29-31 (Again try to express it in your own words; if you are in any doubt about the truth of this, take a careful look at today's news.)

    (b)   What is your response to the statement of Romans 2:1?

> "A promise is not enough; we need a contract. Doors are not enough, we have to lock and bolt them. The payment of fares is not enough, tickets have to be issued, inspected and collected. Law and order are not enough, we need police to enforce them. All this is due to man's sin. We cannot trust each other. We need protection against one another." [16]

Q10 Many argue that the evils of society will disappear as the result of social and political reforms. Though these are needed, are they really at the root of the problem? Consider James 4:1-2 and Mark 7:21-23. Where does the problem originate?

| "Some say 'I have my faults, but at the bottom, I have a good heart.' Alas! It is this that deceives you, for your heart is the worst part of you." [17]

Sin and its consequences

Q11 How would you define sin?

| "What wrong have we done? What sin have we committed against the Lord our God? ... 'all of you are following the stubbornness of your evil hearts instead of obeying me.'" (Jeremiah 16:10,12)

Q12 Who has sinned? Romans 3:23

Q13 | "Sin is not harmful because it is forbidden, but forbidden because it is harmful." [18]

What are some of the consequences of sin?

John 8:34

Ephesians 4:18-19

Hebrews 3:13

James 1:14-15

| "There is a way that appears to be right, but in the end it leads to death." (Proverbs 14:12)

Q14   How will God eventually deal with sin? Revelation 20:11-15 and Matthew 13:40-42

Is there any way out?

Q15   Read Luke 18:9-14.

(a)   What do you think Jesus is saying in this passage?

(b)   What attitude will not help us, and to what must we appeal?

Q16   Read John 3:16-21.

(a)   How does God demonstrate his love and mercy?

(b)   How may we benefit?

(c)   What is the result of rejecting God's offer?

A person is lost not just because they have sinned, but because they have rejected God's remedy for sin, Jesus Christ.

> "For I take no pleasure in the death of anyone, declares the Sovereign Lord. Repent and live!"
> (Ezekiel 18:32)

Further reading

- Vaughan Roberts, *God's Big Design: Life as He Intends It to Be* (IVP, 2013)
- Derek Leaf, *Godfulness* (Navigators UK, 2017)
- Rick Warren, *The Purpose Driven Life: What on Earth Am I Here For?* (Zondervan, 2012)
- Francis Chan and John Piper, *Thinking. Loving. Doing.* (IVP, 2011)

[12] Francis A. Schaeffer, *Death in the City* (Crossway, 2002)

[13] *Westminster Shorter Catechism* (see 1 Corinthians 10:31, Romans 11:36, Psalm 73:25-28)

[14] G.K. Chesterton, quoted in John Blanchard, *Right with God* (The Banner of Truth Trust, 1996)

[15] Aldous Huxley, quoted in Michael Green, *Runaway World* (IVP, 1969)

[16] John Stott, *Basic Christianity* (IVP, 2013)

[17] Charles H. Spurgeon, *The Salt-Cellars* (Delmarva, 2013)

[18] Benjamin Franklin

Richard's Story

My first Bible contained a picture of Noah's ark floating near some rapids, where terrified people were clinging to rocks. You'd think I would have been put off the Bible for life. Not a bit of it. I was enthralled. Who was this Being who had judged the world? What had these people done to deserve such a fate? And the stories kept coming.

The Bible is first and foremost a story-book. As human beings, we live and breathe stories. This grand narrative, 66 books by forty authors, it made sense of my world. The Bible, I discovered, is the Big Story which grounds all other stories.

As I became an adult, I longed to know that my life wouldn't just expire like a firework. Life certainly felt meaningful. The Bible confirmed this. I longed for peace and justice. How could we long for these if they didn't actually exist? The Bible offers Hope: God will put our broken world back together.

Lastly, I wanted what we all want: real, satisfying Love. That's where the Bible really delivered. "There is no greater love than to lay down one's life for one's friends." I discovered that God's Son gave up his life for me. Because he loved me.

The Bible is a story about a God of love, whose beauty and holiness can only be seen through the prism of sacrificial love. It's not just a 'good book'. It's a book that can

Christct

"God was reconciling the world to himself in Christ"
(2 Corinthians 5:19)

"I am the light of the world. Whoever follows me will never walk in darkness, but will have the light of life." (John 8:12)

Who or what is Jesus Christ? A great man, a prophet, a political idealist, a myth? Or is he the Son of God, who came to save the world?

The teaching and claims of Jesus Christ

If you are not familiar with the life and teaching of Jesus Christ, you might want to start with some background reading:

Mark 1:14 – 3:19 tells of the beginning of Jesus' ministry

Luke 10:25 – 12:31 gives a sample of his teaching

Or you could get a better overall picture by reading the whole of Mark's Gospel, which takes about an hour.

 What did Jesus Christ claim about himself?

Mark 14:61-62

John 8:56-58

John 10:30-33

John 14:6

"A man who was merely a man and said the sort of things Jesus said would not be a great moral teacher. He would either be a lunatic – on a level with the man who says he is a poached egg – or else he would be the Devil of Hell. You must make your choice. Either this man was, and is, the Son of God; or else a madman or something worse. You can shut Him up for a fool, you can spit at Him and kill Him as a demon; or you can fall at His feet and call Him Lord and God. But let us not come with any patronising nonsense about His being a great human teacher. He has not left that open to us. He did not intend to." [19]

Q2 What did Jesus claim to do for others?

> Luke 7:48-49

> John 8:31-32, 36

> John 10:27-28

Q3 (a) To what did Jesus point as evidence for his claims? John 10:37-38

(b) What were some of his works?

> Matthew 14:19-21

> Mark 4:39-41

> Luke 7:20-23

> John 11:43-44

Q4   (a)   How did the people who knew Jesus best describe him?

         John 1:14

         1 Peter 2:22

> "The essence of love is self-sacrifice. The worst of men is adorned by an occasional flash of such nobility, but the life of Jesus irradiated it with a never-fading incandescent glow. Jesus was sinless because He was selfless. Such selflessness is love. And God is love." [20]

    (b)   What did his enemies say about him? Mark 14:55-64 and John 19:4-7

> "It seems to me obvious that [Jesus] was neither a lunatic nor a fiend; and consequently, however strange or terrifying or unlikely it may seem, I have to accept the view that He was and is God. God has landed on this enemy occupied world in human form." [21]

The death of Christ

But if Christ's claims are true, then what about his death? Why did he allow it to happen? What does it mean?

Q5   Jesus knew he was going to be put to death. Why didn't he avoid it?

         Mark 9:30-32

         John 10:17-18

         Matthew 20:28

Read Mark 15:1-39 for an account of Jesus' death. You may also like to read Psalm 22 and Isaiah 53, which speak of the death of Christ hundreds of years before the event.

Q6   Read 1 Peter 3:18.

    (a)   Why did Christ die?

(b)   For whom did Christ die?

God is a just and holy God and he will not simply overlook sin or pretend it is something else. In God's eyes, sin is a capital offence!

> "For everyone belongs to me… The one who sins is the one who will die." (Ezekiel 18:4)

The sin and guilt offerings of the Old Testament were a pointer to Jesus Christ's death on the cross. They were a constant reminder to the Jewish people of the terrible consequences of sin. To receive forgiveness for sin, Jews would lay their hands on the head of an unblemished animal and confess their sin – representing a transfer of their sin to the animal. They would then kill the animal and give the blood to the priest. The pouring out or sprinkling of the blood covered the sin, the innocent animal having died in place of the guilty sinner.

Q7   What then is the significance of John the Baptist's description of Jesus in John 1:29?

> "But he was pierced for our transgressions, he was crushed for our iniquities; the punishment that brought us peace was on him, and by his wounds we are healed. We all, like sheep, have gone astray, each of us has turned to our own way; and the Lord has laid on him the iniquity of us all." (Isaiah 53:5-6)

Q8   What did Jesus do to take away sin?

Isaiah 53:5-6 (see above)

1 Peter 2:24

Matthew 26:28

Q9   Is there any other way to obtain forgiveness? Hebrews 9:22

In giving his Son to die for our sin in our place, God has demonstrated for all time that he hates sin but loves us, the sinners.

Jesus Christ is alive today

> "Christ has died:
> Christ is risen:
> Christ will come again." [22]

Q10 Compare Acts 2:22-24 (the first Christian sermon) and 1 Corinthians 15:3-4. What is the main theme of the Christian message?

(For further details of Jesus Christ's resurrection, see Luke 24:1-53 or the first study in this series on Truth.)

Q11 Since Jesus Christ has risen from the dead, what is he now able to do?

Matthew 28:20

Hebrews 7:25

Revelation 1:18

The founders of all other religions are dead or will die, but the founder of Christianity, Jesus Christ, is alive today and forever.

Q12 (a) What did Jesus say will happen one day? Matthew 16:27 and Matthew 24:30

(b) When will this happen? Matthew 24:36

(c) What are we encouraged to do? Matthew 24:44

Whether we are still alive when Jesus Christ returns or whether we die before then, we are wise to be ready.

Q13   (a)   Compare John 8:24 with Acts 10:43. Does everyone benefit from what Christ has done?

(b)   How can we be sure of benefiting?

(c)   What is true for those who trust in Christ?

(d)   What is true for those who don't?

"Salvation is found in no one else, for there is no other name under heaven given to mankind by which we must be saved." (Acts 4:12)

Further reading

- The Gospels: Matthew, Mark, Luke and John
- John Piper, *Seeing and Savouring Jesus Christ* (IVP, 2005)
- John Stott, *Basic Christianity* (IVP, 2013)
- C.S. Lewis, *Miracles* (William Collins, 2016)

19 C.S. Lewis, *Mere Christianity* (William Collins, 2016)
20 John Stott, *Basic Christianity* (IVP, 2013)
21 C.S. Lewis, *Mere Christianity* (William Collins, 2016)
22 Holy Communion, *Common Worship* (Church of England, 2000)

Kash's Story

My father attended church on special occasions but my mom attended church with the kids every Sunday. As a child, I loved Sundays and had a desire for God I cannot really explain. When I was eight years old, I came to hear and appreciate on some level that Jesus Christ died for me.

Fast forward a few years to when I turned 18 and wondered again what the relevance of his death was. Why did he have to die? After many discussions and reading the Bible, I understood that he was my proxy. Jesus sacrificed his life with God so I could also have life with God, if I believed that this sacrifice really happened.

Every religion except Christianity is centred around good works. Jesus offers us everything for free, and I do not need to do anything good or bad to qualify for his love. I've learnt that good works do not make a person a Christian. Humanity is fundamentally flawed, and we do not have what it takes to be good in and of ourselves.

Jesus gave me his life and has loved me unconditionally, not on the basis of my character but in a way that is without measure. The love of God is amazing. It is liberating. It is comforting. It is hope in the hard times. Because I have God, I will never be without help, and I am certain and secure in the fact that after life on earth ends, I will spend eternity with him. He is worth it. It is the best decision I have made in my entire life.

Trust

"...it is the power of God that brings salvation to everyone who believes" (Romans 1:16)

"The disciples ...were greatly astonished and asked, 'Who then can be saved?' Jesus looked at them and said, 'With man this is impossible, but with God all things are possible.'" (Matthew 19:25-26)

People's most basic and fundamental need is to be saved or rescued from their sin and its terrible consequences, and brought back into a right relationship with God. How can this happen? What must a person do to be saved in this way? And how is such a person different as a result?

The problem and the solution

 Read Romans 3:19-28. This passage contains several words which are not used every day, but are key to unlocking its meaning. Some definitions may be helpful:

The law	God's moral law as summarised in the Ten Commandments (see v 19, 20, 28)
Justify	To declare innocent, to acquit. It is the translation of a Greek word that comes from the same stem as the word that is translated 'righteous' or 'just' (see v 24, 26 and 28)
Grace	Unmerited favour (see v 24)
Redemption	The "act of buying a slave out of bondage in order to set him free" [23] (see v 24)
Atonement	The penalty that God has paid on our behalf, to bring us back into relationship with him (see v 25)

(a)   How does Paul describe humanity's problem? (v 19, 20, 23)

(b)   Is it possible for us to earn God's love and why/why not?

How are we put right with God? (21-26)

> "Faith… is that simple and openhearted attitude to God which takes Him at His word and gratefully accepts His grace." [24]

Q2 Consider Ephesians 2:8-9 and Titus 3:5.

(a) According to these verses, what is not the basis for a person being saved?

(b) On what basis is a person saved?

A new beginning

God has provided the perfect solution to our greatest problem through the life, death and resurrection of Jesus Christ. But not everyone has discovered it, so many are still separated from God.

Q3 (a) What is needed for God's answer to sin to become real in a person's life and experience? John 3:3

(b) Who gives this new birth? John 1:12-13

(c) How is it given? John 1:12

Q4 Look at the following passages and for each one answer the two questions below.

What response are we encouraged to make?

What does God promise?

John 5:24

Acts 2:38

Acts 3:19

Acts 10:43

The passages above talk about the great turning point in a person's life that we might call becoming a Christian. It is a change so radical in its consequences that Jesus Christ described it as being born again, or being born of the Spirit (John 3:3-15). In other places in the Bible it is described as 'turning to God' (1 Thessalonians 1:9), 'coming to Christ' (John 6:37), 'receiving Christ' (Colossians 2:6) or simply 'believing' (Acts 14:1).

Becoming a Christian involves a response of the whole person (mind, heart and will) to God's love in Christ. The section at the end of this study explains what this response might look like.

Q5   Read Romans 10:9-13.

(a)   How is becoming a Christian described in this passage?

(b)   What is true of the person who does this?

(c)   Is it possible for a person to know that they are saved?

The confidence that I have because I trust in Christ is not determined by the greatness of my faith, but by the greatness of the One in whom my faith rests.

"God is not human, that he should lie, not a human being, that he should change his mind. Does he speak and then not act? Does he promise and not fulfill?" (Numbers 23:19)

A new life and a new lifestyle

Jesus described becoming a Christian as a new birth, and a new birth marks the beginning of a new life.

Q6 How does Paul describe the person who has come to faith in Christ? 2 Corinthians 5:17

Q7 What are we told about the Christian in the following verses?

   Romans 5:1

   1 Corinthians 1:9

   1 Corinthians 6:19-20

   1 Peter 1:3-4

Q8 (a) What are some of the changes you might expect to see in the life of someone who has become a Christian?

   Colossians 3:5-15

   (b) What does Jesus expect from his followers?

   Matthew 10:32

   Luke 9:23

It is important to realise that it is not the change in a person's behaviour that makes them a Christian. The change in their relationship with God makes them a Christian and the changes in their behaviour are a result of that.

"How will I keep it up?" is a question many people have faced as they have considered becoming a Christian. But what does the Bible say?

> Jude 24

> Romans 8:37-39

> 1 Corinthians 10:13

"You can become a Christian in a moment, but not a mature Christian. Christ can enter and cleanse and forgive you in a matter of seconds, but it may take a lifetime for your character to be transformed and moulded to his will." [25]

 What are some of the resources that God has given the Christian to enable them to live a new life?

> John 14:26

> Philippians 4:6-7

> Acts 20:32

> Acts 2:42

"Enter through the narrow gate. For wide is the gate and broad is the road that leads to destruction, and many enter through it. But small is the gate and narrow the road that leads to life, and only a few find it." (Matthew 7:13-14)

Becoming a Christian

> "What shall I do, then, with Jesus who is called the Messiah?" (Matthew 27:22)

This is a question asked by Pontius Pilate, Procurator of Judea c. 27 AD. It is a question to which we must all give an answer, either as a conscious response or by conscious or unconscious neglect. Having studied something of what the Bible says about Jesus Christ and becoming a Christian, it would be good for you to pause at this point and think about your own position before God.

Consider that you will one day face God as your judge. Consider also the death and resurrection of Jesus Christ which make it possible for you to be made right with God.

> "How shall we escape if we ignore so great a salvation?" (Hebrews 2:3)

Consider Revelation 3:20. As Jesus Christ stands at the 'door' of your life:

What is he doing?

What must you do to have Christ enter your life?

When you do this, what is his promise?

If, as you consider, you believe that you have sinned against God, but that Jesus Christ can take away your sin and make you right with him, and if you are willing to turn from all that you know to be wrong to follow Christ, we suggest you express this repentance and faith in prayer.

You may like to pray this prayer:

> "Lord Jesus, I know that I am a sinner, guilty and unable to save myself, lost and unable to find my way to the Father without you, but I know too that you love me in spite of my sin. I believe that you are God's Son, and that you died for my sin and rose from the dead. I turn from my sins, asking you to forgive them and to come into my life as Saviour and Lord. Please give me the grace to follow you and to live a new life."

> "Everyone who calls on the name of the Lord will be saved." (Romans 10:13)

Further reading

- The Gospel of John, which was "written that you may believe that Jesus is the Messiah, the Son of God, and that by believing you may have life in his name" (John 20:31)
- John Piper, *Don't Waste Your Life* (IVP, 2005)
- Vaughan Roberts, *Turning Points* (Authentic Media, 2001)
- John Blanchard, *Right with God* (The Banner of Truth Trust, 1996)
- John Stott, *Basic Christianity* (IVP, 2013)

[23] F.F. Bruce, *Romans* (IVP, 2008)
[24] F.F. Bruce, *Romans* (IVP, 2008)
[25] John Stott, *Basic Christianity* (IVP, 2013)

Thompy's Story

I grew up in Northern Ireland as a good church-going Protestant. There was no good reason to doubt that Jesus was God's Son and the Bible was true. It felt right culturally.

It was years later that some Christian friends, who I thought I agreed with faith-wise, unsettled me with how they practised their religion. Their faith profoundly influenced their identity and behaviour. I concluded that, if I was saying that Jesus was Creator and Lord, then he ought to rule every area of my life. He deserved the same place in my heart as God gave him in the universe. I began to change; then I went to England!

Pursuing a career in the army, I entered a boarding college. My life changed dramatically and my Christian resolve fell apart. I took two years to realise it. When I finally repented and plucked up the courage to tell my best friend, he was dumbstruck, unable to accept it. You might imagine my shame; I felt a totally failed Christian.

I realised that, if this 'faith' thing was going to work for me, I needed help. I joined a few others to study the Bible. I began to realise how God wanted a personal relationship with me, made possible by Jesus' death on the cross. He didn't want to relate to me as a commanding officer who issued orders, but as a loving Father who invited me to get to know him in a way I could never merit – I just needed to accept it. It was a lesson I learnt that day, and have been learning every day since, which revolutionised my life.